# BIG BUBBLEFACTS

# Hysterical Britain

Miles Kelly
PUBLISHING

First published in 2006 by
Miles Kelly Publishing Ltd
Bardfield Centre, Great Bardfield, Essex, CM7 4SL

Copyright © Miles Kelly Publishing Ltd 2006

2 4 6 8 10 9 7 5 3 1

Publishing Director: Anne Marshall

Senior Editor: Belinda Gallagher

Art Director Jo Brewer

Designer: Louisa Leitao

Production: Elizabeth Brunwin

ISBN 1-84236-674-2

Reprographics: Anthony Cambray, Mike Coupe, Stephan Davis, Ian Paulyn

Printed in China

British Library Cataloguing-in-Publication Data
A catalogue record for this book is available from the British Library

Cartoons: Mark Davis

Indexer: Jane Parker

www.mileskelly.net
info@mileskelly.net

# Contents

# ROMAN INVADERS

# Celtic clans

## enemies of Rome

The people who lived in Great Britain during Roman times were called Britons. Their language and way of life is known as 'Celtic'. The Celtic people lived right across Europe, from Spain to Turkey. Other Celts included the Gaels of Ireland and the Gauls of France.

DUCK!

WHERE?

NOW WITH CENTRAL HEATING!

WHOOSH!

OINK!

Most Britons lived in small settlements of large, round houses made of clay, timber and stone.

The Britons belonged to many different tribes. They were always fighting among themselves, and each tribe had its own king or queen and its own lands. There were important nobles, too, including priests and law-makers called druids. Most Britons were farmers and many others were blacksmiths and ironworkers.

Clothes were woven from linen and wool, and cloaks were fastened at the shoulder. Britons also liked wearing gold jewellery and the Romans thought they were show-offs, forever boasting about how brave they were. Women wore long dresses and men wore tunics and trousers.

Celtic warriors fought with long spears and swords, and used horse-drawn chariots for speedy attacks.

# Britons attacked

## Roman rampage

In 55BC, a Roman fleet carrying 10,000 men approached the cliffs of Dover. Their commander, Julius Caesar, wanted to punish the Britons because they'd been supporting the Gauls, who had been fighting against him. Soon after the Romans came ashore, a storm blew up, damaging their ships. Caesar decided to sail home.

The first Roman to wade ashore was the standard bearer of the Tenth Legion. The other troops followed.

In AD42 the Roman emperor Claudius put together an army of over 40,000 men. Its aim was to bring the whole of Britain under Roman rule, once and for all. In the spring of AD43, Roman troops finally landed in Kent, led by General Aulus Plautius.

When ordered to invade Britain in AD43, the Roman troops went on strike, as they thought the Channel shore was the edge of the human world!

STONE THE HENGE! MEN IN SKIRTS!

YUK!

QUICK! LEG IT LADS!

CALLING ALL CELTS... RUN FOR YOUR LIVES!

PUFF

The Romans broke through the ranks of tribes and captured Colchester. Eleven tribes finally surrendered.

# Celtic rebels
## killer queen

In their first summer in Britain, the Romans made a big mistake. They captured Caratacus, son of a Celtic king. However, he escaped and joined tribes in Wales where he led many attacks on the Romans. When Caratacus was finally defeated in AD51, he fled to the Brigantes tribe. The queen of the Brigantes handed him back to the Romans.

Caratacus escaped, but was handed back to the Romans. He was taken to Rome as a prisoner of war.

In AD60 the Romans attacked the druids (Celtic priests) of Mona. They were all slaughtered.

Boudicca, queen of the Iceni, attacked Colchester, London and St Albans. She was eventually defeated.

# Rule Britannia
## a new era

**Britain became 'Britannia'.** It was now a province of the mighty Roman empire, with its capital at Londinium, and was ruled by a governor. The province was divided into territories, military settlements and towns. Each had a council and elected magistrates to enforce the law.

The Roman army kept control. They set up military camps and strong forts built of timber and stone.

More Britons took up Roman customs. In the countryside, the old Celtic way of life carried on as before.

Many Romans moved to Britannia from Italy. They included doctors, servants and upper-class ladies.

# Hitting the road
## take a hike

**The Romans introduced the first planned road system in Britain.** Some were minor routes, but others were up to 12 metres wide, straight and well-drained. The chief purpose of these roads was to allow legions of soldiers to march quickly from one part of the country to another. No better roads were built until the 1800s.

The most important travellers were official messengers who rode on horseback. They travelled at speed.

Roads were made with whatever stone was locally available. Layers of broken flint and stone were laid as foundations. The surface was generally gravel, but it was sometimes paved. Roads were built by the army, using troops or slaves as labour.

Slow traffic would move onto the broad verges to let faster traffic, such as messengers, go by. Some travellers used fast, lightweight carts pulled by mules, while others rode in slower, horse-drawn carriages. Heavy goods were carried in wooden wagons hauled by teams of oxen.

I TOLD YOU — NO MEAD ON THE JOB!

BZZ!

BZZ!

IT'S ONLY SHANDY OCCIFER...

SWOOSH!

STONE ME!

The roads were centred around Londinium (London). Most branched out to important army towns.

# Hustle and bustle
## city life

**The Romans built grand towns, often on the sites of Celtic capitals.** Smaller towns sprung up around crossroads and rivers, as well as by the sea. Roman officials, traders, lawyers and craftsmen moved in first, followed by Britons who could afford to take up the Roman way of life.

DUMPED!

The Roman period saw the first proper towns in Britain, with paved streets and grid-planned housing.

London (Londinium) was sited on the banks of the river Thames, ideally placed for trade with the empire. A long wooden bridge spanned the river, and the city had a huge fort, town hall and market place. At its peak, Londinium had a population of around 45,000 people.

When Boudicca rebelled, Roman troops had to march at very high speed. They covered 400 kilometres in 14 days!

COME ON LADIES, YOU KNOW IT MAKES SENSE!

SNAP!

LOOKS GREAT IN ANY VILLA...

Towns were supplied with water by aqueducts (water channels). Drains and sewers kept towns clean.

The Romans worshipped many gods and goddesses. Jupiter was king of the gods, Venus was goddess of love, Mercury was messenger of the gods, Diana was goddess of hunting, and Saturn was god of farming. Every Roman knew stories about the gods. In these stories, gods would act like people – quarrelling and falling in love.

Beautiful temples were built so that people could make offerings and give thanks to the gods.

Mithras was the Persian god of light and he was very popular among Roman troops. He was often depicted slaying a bull. Many temples were built to honour Mithras, including one in London.

In the countryside, the Britons still worshipped the Celtic gods and goddesses. In fact, many Romans happily adopted these gods, too. This was because they were often similar to their own gods. They even built shrines to many of them.

Foreign religions grew popular in Britannia over the years. Some emperors were even worshipped as gods.

**Great Britain formed the northwestern frontier of the Roman empire.** The Romans never conquered Ireland, so most of the frontier followed the coastline. In the north of Britain however, it crossed the land, and was defended by a wall – Hadrian's Wall. Its aim was to keep out tribes on the northern side and stop them from making alliances with tribes on the southern side.

There were forts along the wall to guard crossing points. Patrols brought in tribe members for questioning

Emperor Hadrian gave his name to the great northern wall, which was begun in AD122. For the soldiers serving there, life must have been boring. When troops weren't building or digging, they had marches, weapons-training or drill on parade. In their spare time they hunted, gambled or wrote letters home.

he wall was about 4 metres high by 3 metres wide. It was defended by ditches and ran for 117 kilometres.

# Home from home
### luxury villas

**Villas were large Roman country houses.** They were usually built at the centre of a large estate, with orchards and fields of wheat, flocks of sheep or herds of cattle. Labour was provided by slaves. Villa owners were usually wealthy Romans, such as government officials or retired army officers, but some Britons also owned land.

The first villas were simple farmhouses, but as Rome prospered they became more and more luxurious.

The estates also offered hunting with dogs. Deer were a popular choice as venison was often a welcome addition to the menu. Boar (wild pig) were common in Britain, and could become very dangerous if cornered. A charging boar could send a hunter flying and its sharp tusks could gash a leg badly.

Villa floors were decorated with mosaics, which are pictures made up of hundreds (or thousands) of tiny tiles, set in cement, to make pictures and patterns. It was common to see images of gods in these mosaics, as well as animals or fruit. Craftsmen would travel the empire laying mosaics.

ouses and gardens were decorated with shrines to the gods. It was believed these protected the household.

# Hard day's work

## the daily grind

**Britons were famous for their pottery before the arrival of the Romans.** However, under Roman rule, pottery-making became a big industry. The design of kilns (where pottery was 'fired' and hardened) improved greatly, and before long, dishes, jugs and kitchenware were being produced on a large scale.

Potteries sprung up wherever there was good clay. There were many in Oxfordshire and southern England.

The Romans could teach the Celts little about ironworking or blacksmithing, as it was their speciality. Business boomed as there was always work to be done – armour, weapons, axes, pans and horseshoes all needed making!

Roman ships have been found preserved in the mud of the river Thames. London's first wharves have also been discovered.

HOW'S THINGS?

SEW SEW...

PERFECT FOR THAT SPECIAL TOGA.

MUNCH

SMITH BY NAME... TRADE...

Weaving was a big industry under Roman rule. Work was done by hand, as there were no spinning wheels.

# Learning and medicine
## Roman style

**The children of wealthier Britons and Romans went to school at age six or seven.** At school they would learn reading, writing, history, sport and arithmetic. Most children left school around the age of 11 and some continued education at home.

At school, lessons would usually be very boring, and tutors would often hit students for wrong answers!

Girls would be expected to learn weaving and how to run a household as training for married life.

Medicine was basic, but doctors still treated eye infections and carried out operations.

# Time to relax

## when in Rome...

**Every town had a public bath.**
Even wealthier Britons enjoyed bathing, too. Men and women bathed separately. People went to get clean, relax, have a massage or just chat with their friends. Any fair-sized town also had an open-air theatre where plays and gladiator fights were held.

Bathers covered their bodies in oil, then scraped themselves clean. Gladiators were slaves or prisoners.

The Romans loved playing games and gambling. The clatter of rolling dice could be heard in bath houses, inns and barrack rooms around Britannia. Playing boards were usually made of pottery, with little gaming pieces of bone, glass, clay or ivory.

Chariot-racers had the same following of fans as football stars do today. Everyone followed their favourite team!

GOOD SHOT!

SMACK!

WHOOSHHH!

CHECK-MATE!

OOPS... THAT'S BLOWN IT!

A popular game was 'Three Stones', which was like noughts and crosses. Children liked playing ball games.

# Togas and jewels
## looking good!

**The most common Roman dress was a simple tunic, worn by workers, slaves and children.** A woollen cloak would sometimes be worn for warmth. Important men wore a white robe called a toga, and men of high rank wore a purple-trimmed toga.

Hairstyles went in and out of fashion. Men usually had short styles. Women curled and plaited their hair.

Women wore lipstick, eyeshadow and face powder. Rich ladies wore jewellery of gold and pearl.

People wore sandals. Soldiers wore sandals with studded soles for marching. Boots were worn in winter.

# Eating and drinking

## Roman cuisine

**Roman kitchens had ovens for baking bread, hearths for boiling and spits for roasting.** Oil and other foods were stored in large pottery jars. Hung up in the kitchen you might find a hare or a duck. Spread out on the tables would be herbs, spices and vegetables.

Breakfast was usually just bread or fruit. Lunch might be leftovers from the night before.

## Can you believe it?

A Roman banquet might include odd dishes such as moray eel, dormice, bear cutlets, sow's udders, or poached snails!

At a Roman banquet, guests would eat lying on couches around a low table. Servants would bring in seven or eight courses. There would be starters, salads, dumplings, omelettes and shellfish. Main dishes consisted of kidneys, liver, roast venison in plum sauce or young goat cooked in cream.

Romans and wealthy Britons would have their wine imported from Italy, Gaul and Germany.

# KINGS AND QUEENS

# Warrior queen

## Roman riots

**Queen Boudicca rebelled against the Romans.** In AD61, she led an army of Celtic tribes to attack Roman towns. After several Celtic successes, the Romans fought back and defeated the Celts. Rather than surrender, Queen Boudicca took deadly poison and died.

Queen Boudicca led her Celtic army into battle against the Romans and burned down London.

## can you believe it?

The Celts were show-offs! Warriors sometimes wore their hair in spikes, tattooed their skin, and wore gold jewellery!

When they stormed a Celtic fort, the Roman army would often form a 'tortoise'. This formation was made by soldiers lifting their shields above their heads. Spears and rocks thrown by the enemy would bounce off the tortoise 'shell'.

The Romans were stopped in their tracks for a while. They eventually fought back and defeated the Celts.

# Viking invaders

## fighting for power

**Cnut the Great was a powerful Viking ruler.** He was king of Denmark, Norway and England from 1016 to 1035. Although he was harsh, Cnut claimed to be a good Christian. He used his power as king to bring peace, which lasted until he died.

King Cnut tried to command the waves. Eric Bloodaxe was ruler of York. Enemies forced him to leave.

Sigurd the Stout ruled many Scottish islands between AD985 and 1014. He had a flag with a picture of a raven on it, which he thought would always make him victorious in battle. But Sigurd was eventually defeated.

In 1165, Malcolm IV of Scotland died because he went without food to show his devotion to God.

IT IS A MAGIC FLAG. IT IS, IT IS IT IS!

YEAH OK!!

LONG HAIR IS BANNED!

PITY BIG MOUTHS AREN'T!

Sigurd the Stout thought a flag was magic. Thorfinn the Mighty planned new ways to rule the Orkney Islands.

# Quarrels and fights

## moody kings!

Henry II was strong and very determined. He passed many strict laws – but he couldn't make his wife, Eleanor of Aquitaine, obey him! In 1173 she led a rebellion against her husband because of the way he was ruling her family's lands in France. Henry imprisoned her for life.

Henry II sent his wife to prison. He argued with Thomas Becket, a Church leader, who was then murdered.

Richard the Lionheart was cruel to his enemies. John I had to sign a document giving people more rights.

Henry III owned Britain's first zoo. He spent his last years planning a new cathedral – Westminster Abbey.

# Temper temper!

## revolting monarchs

### Edward I was the tallest king.

He was given the nickname 'Longshanks' meaning long legs, as he was over 2 metres tall! Edward was also very hot-tempered. He once tore out his son's hair in a fury and broke his daughter's coronet!

NICE PAD!

LOSE MY TEMPER? ME?

CHILL OUT.

OH NO. BIG MISTAKE.

I DO, I DO, I DO!

SHE'S KEEN!

Edward I had a furious temper. The wife of Edward II was nicknamed 'She-wolf'! She ran away to France.

When Edward I was stabbed with a poisoned dagger, people say that his wife saved him by sucking out the poison.

In 1348 a terrible disease called the Black Death reached England. victims developed a cough, high fever and boils on their bodies. Almost half the population of England died. At the time, no one knew what caused the disease. Today, we know that it was caused by rat fleas.

FIRE!

PING!

NOT AS EASY AS IT LOOKS...

TOO YOUNG TO RIDE INTO BATTLE! PHEW!

SPLUTTER!

he Hundred Years War between England and France was started by Edward III. Richard II was a teenage king!

# Killer kings

## plots and intrigue

**Edward IV was a brave fighter.** He became king in 1461 and proved to be a clever army commander and politician. But Edward could be ruthless. In his search for power he gave orders for Henry VI to be murdered. When he suspected his brother of plotting against him, he ordered for him to be drowned.

Edward IV liked food, drink and pretty women. When he died, his sons were put in the Tower of London.

Richard III died in battle in 1485. He wore his crown as he fought, and was an easy target for the enemy.

Bad stories about Richard III may have been written by Sir Thomas More, who worked for the Tudors.

# Times are changing
## Tudor capers

THIS PEN IS RUBBISH!

I AM THE KING, HONEST.

HMM, YOU LOOK MORE LIKE MY UNCLE HARRY...

WHO?

HE'S AN IMPOSTER!

**Henry VII founded a new ruling family – the Tudors.** He was the son of a Welsh lord and an English noblewoman. Although Henry had only a weak claim to be king, after killing Richard III in battle, he brought peace to England.

Henry VII united England. When he died in 1509 the country was richer than it had been for many years.

48

Henry VIII had six wives. He wanted a son, so he divorced or beheaded many wives until he had his heir.

Henry formed his own church and closed many monasteries. He also set up the first modern navy.

**Elizabeth I decided not to get married.** Her mother was Anne Boleyn, the second wife of Henry VIII – and the first to be beheaded. Not getting married meant that Elizabeth didn't have to share her power. When she died in 1603, the Tudor line came to an end.

Elizabeth I refused to marry. In 1588 she gave a speech to her troops when a Spanish fleet attacked.

Elizabeth I had her own personal pirate. He was Sir Francis Drake, a brilliant sailor who was the first Englishman to sail around the world. He made many pirate attacks, especially on ships sailing back to Spain.

Queen Elizabeth I would send priests to prison for wearing the wrong clothes!

YOUR TREASURE OR YOUR LIFE!

YOU'RE SO DEMANDING...

BE OVER IN A SECOND...

HOPE THIS AXE IS SHARP!

Drake shared his pirate treasure with the queen. Elizabeth ordered Mary Queen of Scots to be executed.

# Stormin' Normans!
## conquest!

In 1066 William the Conqueror killed King Harold at the Battle of Hastings. William was from Normandy in France. He began to build castles as soon as he was king.

The Normans built simple 'motte and bailey' castles. Each had a wooden tower, standing on a tall earth mound called a 'motte'. This was then surrounded by a tall wooden fence. Early castles were used as army bases.

Workers dug a deep ditch called a moat around the outside of the castle, to stop attackers getting in.

The first castles were brought to England by sea. The Normans made them in sections from wood, before they invaded in 1066. These were then loaded onto their battle ships. When they arrived in England, the Normans put the castles together.

For extra protection the wooden planks that made up the fence were sharpened into points.

# When a king lost... his head!

**James VI and James I were the same man!** Already the sixth king of Scotland, James became the first king to rule both England and Scotland. He ruled each country separately – the two did not become a united kingdom until 1707.

James hated smoking and wrote a book about its dangers. But he was foolishly fond of some silly friends.

Charles I thought he was chosen by God to be king. But he argued with Parliament and started a civil war.

The Roundheads supported Parliament and the Cavaliers supported the king. In 1648 Charles was executed.

Royal goings-on!
*great pretenders*

**Although German, George I had a claim to the English throne.** He also preferred to speak German or French. King of England, Scotland and Wales from 1714 to 1727, George was the great grandson of James I. He also locked his wife, Dorothea, away in a castle when she became friends with a handsome nobleman.

George I was furious with his wife, and locked her up. Riding into battle in 1743, George II fell off his hors

## can you believe it?

George II died while visiting the closet (royal lavatory). He collapsed from a heart attack and died there.

Bonnie Prince Charlie was called the 'Young Pretender'. He claimed to be the rightful English and Scottish king. When he invaded Scotland in 1745 his attack went well. His army marched towards London but was forced to retreat by the English soldiers. After the Battle of Culloden, Charlie spent many weeks in hiding until Flora MacDonald helped him to escape.

Bonnie Prince Charlie's army was massacred by the English at the Battle of Culloden in 1746.

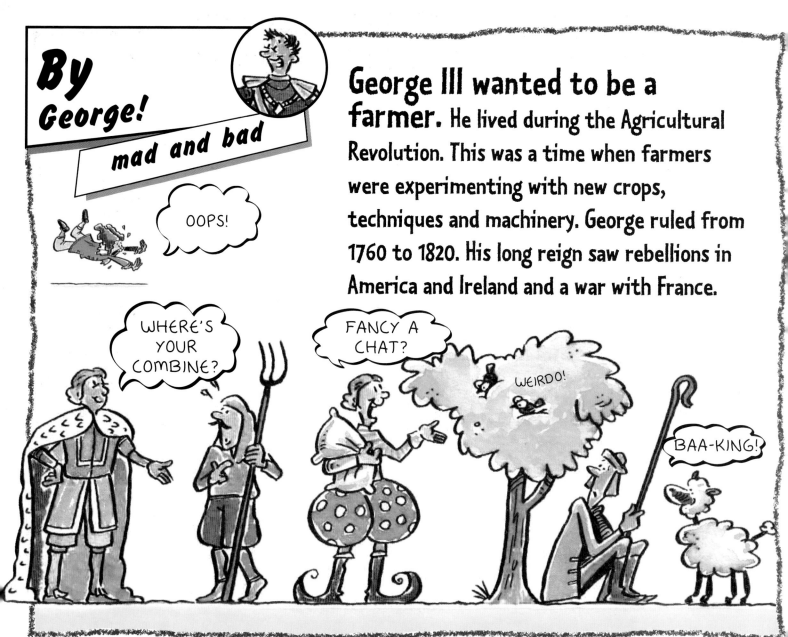

# By George!
### mad and bad

**George III wanted to be a farmer.** He lived during the Agricultural Revolution. This was a time when farmers were experimenting with new crops, techniques and machinery. George ruled from 1760 to 1820. His long reign saw rebellions in America and Ireland and a war with France.

George III liked to talk to the people. But he had spells of mental illness and would talk to trees!

George IV loved drinking, wearing nice clothes – and eating fine food. He didn't take his duties seriously.

In 1830, Parliament wanted to let the people vote. William IV said no, and earned the nickname Silly Billy.

# Bring on the Victorians

## empire builders

**Queen Victoria ruled the largest empire in the world.** She became queen in 1837 and ruled for 64 years. During her reign Britain became a world leader in technology. The arrival of steam-powered ships and locomotives allowed people to travel further afield than ever before.

Queen Victoria married Prince Albert and had nine children. Steam engines helped to transport goods.

Queen Victoria became known as the 'grandmother of Europe'. Because Britain was so powerful, many other European countries wanted to show friendship. So they arranged marriages between Victoria's children and their own.

Like many other British people, Queen Victoria became fascinated by India's cultural heritage and rich civilization. She collected Indian jewels and art treasures and hired an Indian servant to teach her one of India's languages, Hindi.

Amazing bridges and architecture were built in Victoria's reign. The queen became empress of India, too.

# Wartime royals

*stiff upper lip!*

After Queen Victoria died, her son became king as Edward VII. His reign lasted from 1901 until 1910, and Edward proved to be a skilled politician and diplomat. He also spoke many foreign languages very well.

Edward VII also had a fun side and he liked fast cars, horse racing, gambling and sailing.

George V saw the outbreak of World War I in 1914. Edward VIII gave up his throne for love.

George VI didn't want to be king. London was bombed during World War II, but the royals didn't leave.

# Modern times
## Elizabeth II

Elizabeth II has travelled farther than any other British monarch. After 1950, many lands ruled by Britain wanted to be independent. Elizabeth set up a new organization called the Commonwealth. This encouraged former British lands to stay in touch with each other and the monarchy.

Queen Elizabeth II has travelled thousands of miles meeting other Commonwealth people and leaders.

## can you believe it?

George IV was very fat! This earned him the nickname 'Prince of Whales' when he was Prince Regent!

Elizabeth married Prince Philip in 1947. They have four children – Princes Charles, Andrew and Edward – and Princess Anne. When Prince Philip married, one of the new titles he was given was Duke of Edinburgh.

Prince Philip is Queen Elizabeth's husband. He has accompanied her on many of her travels to foreign lands.

# BRITISH HISTORY

# Stone and bronze
## making tools

Human beings first lived in Great Britain about 37,000 years ago. By 6000BC, hunters in Britain had become skilled at making tools such as needles, fish hooks and harpoons. They hunted deer, boar and wild oxen in the oak forests. Animal skins were used to make clothes and they also provided coverings for shelters.

*I HATE SEWING!*

*BLING!*

*TIME TO CATCH DINNER!*

*WHOOSH!*

*YOU'VE BEEN AXED!*

*SWEAT!*

Flint was an excellent stone to make tools with. These razor-sharp tools were used to hunt animals.

Massive pillars of stone were used to create Stonehenge. The stones were positioned so that they lined up with the rising and setting Sun. It is thought that Stonehenge was used to observe the Sun, Moon and stars. People would have crowded into the circle on midsummer morning to watch the rising of the Sun.

DON'T LIKE THE LOOK OF THAT SOUP.

PUT SOME EFFORT INTO IT!

PERSONAL PORTRAITS FOR FREE!

SIZZLE!

Hot, liquid bronze was later used to make metal tools. Stonehenge was built between 3000 and 1500BC.

# Celtic capers

## warriors and forts

Around 600BC, warriors from mainland Europe began to settle in parts of the British Isles. Many of them belonged to a group of people called the Celts. Those people already living in the British Isles slowly adopted the Celtic way of life. They began to speak Celtic languages, too.

Many British Celts lived in villages of large round houses. Most Celts were farmers or blacksmiths.

The Celts were first-rate metal workers. They realized that iron was a hard, useful metal. In fact, people who had not seen iron before thought that it had magical properties. Some people still nail iron horseshoes onto doors for good luck.

The safest place to be when war broke out was on top of a hill! These places were easily defended with ditches and wooden fences.

MIRROR, MIRROR IN MY HAND...

YOU'RE THE UGLIEST IN THE LAND!

YIKES!!

LOSER!

WHERE'S THE BRAKE?

The Celts were show-offs and liked to look good! Chariots and swords were used in times of battle.

**The Romans first came to Britain in 55BC.** However, it was not until AD43 that they conquered most of the land. Only the north of Scotland remained free of Roman rule. In AD122, the Romans built Hadrian's Wall. This marked the northern border of an empire that stretched from Spain, to North Africa, and the Black Sea.

In AD60, Queen Boudicca rebelled against the Romans. She burned down towns, but was eventually defeated

The Romans liked their comforts. Rich people lived in luxurious country houses called villas. These even had under-floor central heating.

Roman soldiers began to leave Britain in AD401. Many parts of the Roman empire were under attack. In Britain there were rebellions. Pirates sailed the seas. The Irish attacked western shores. The city of Rome itself was captured by German warriors in AD476.

The Romans opened public baths where people could have a hot or cold dip. Long, straight roads were built.

# Under attack!

## Anglo-Saxons

**People from Germany began to attack eastern Britain.** More and more of them landed in the 400s and 500s. They belonged to various peoples known as Angles, Saxons, Jutes and Frisians. We call them Anglo-Saxons. Their speech became the English language, mixed with Celtic and Latin.

The Anglo-Saxons slowly conquered the south and east of Britain. They divided it into separate kingdoms.

The first Christians in Britain were Romans. The Anglo-Saxons still worshipped their own gods.

King Alfred ruled the kingdom of Wessex from 871 to 899. His army fought off Danish invaders.

# Viking raiders

## Britain attacked

**The Vikings were pirates, raiders, explorers, traders and farmers.** Some people called them Northmen, or Danes, as their homeland was Norway, Sweden and Denmark. Viking raiders began to attack the British Isles in 789. They were soon feared far and wide.

Viking longships carried warriors inland to towns and villages where they could steal treasure.

The Vikings fought against the Anglo-Saxons and soon controlled large areas of England. In 1016, England even had a Viking king, Cnut I. Vikings also ruled the Isle of Man and large areas of Scotland and Ireland.

## Can you believe it?

Before they went into battle, Viking warriors (berserkirs) worked themselves up into a frenzy. This is where the word 'berserk' comes from.

The Vikings stole livestock and made people slaves. They realized that Britain provided good farmland.

# Norman conquerors

### France attacks

**William, Duke of Normandy, was descended from the Vikings.**
Although William was French, he thought he had a claim to the English throne. In 1066 William crossed the Channel with a fleet of ships. His aim was to become king of England.

William's army met the English in a great battle near Hastings in Sussex.

The Normans created the Domesday Book. In it they recorded the houses and lands in their new kingdom. People had to work for their new Norman lords, and pay taxes. The Domesday Book helped the king to keep track of everything.

English King Harold was killed, and the Normans marched to London. William was crowned king of England.

# Knights and castles

## riding into battle

The Normans began to build castles in Britain. The first castles were made of wood, but before long they were made with thick stone walls and towers. Water-filled ditches called moats surrounded them. Castles were built in Britain for the next 400 years.

The most important soldiers were knights. They practised fighting in mock battles called tournaments.

A knight's armour weighed around 13 kilograms. Add to that the weight of all the weapons – and pity the poor horse!

Each noble family had its own badge called a coat-of-arms. This appeared on shields and flags and helped to show which knight was which during a battle. There were strict rules about the design of coats-of-arms, known as heraldry.

JOLLY GOOD SHOW, BOYS!

COME ON YOU REDS!

Yummy!

WHY ARE WE WEARING TIN CANS ON OUR HEADS?

Banquets were held in the great hall of a castle. Venison (deer), swan and goose were often served.

# Middle Ages

## town life

**Towns were still small in the Middle Ages, and surrounded by high walls.** Streets were narrow, muddy, and smelly, too. Houses and buildings were built from timber, which meant they could catch fire easily.

A market was usually held once a week. During the Middle Ages, many towns were protected by a castle.

Few people could read. Special signs were hung outside shops so that people knew what was being sold. This sign shows that pottery, such as jugs, bowls and pots, is for sale.

Knights and squires on their way to tournaments would stop off in towns to buy food and drink.

# Tudor times...

## ...Stewart, too!

**The Tudors ruled England and Wales after 1485.** They also controlled a small part of Ireland, around Dublin. The Tudor rulers and nobles liked to live in fine palaces rather than draughty castles. The Stewart family ruled Scotland. Their greatest king was James IV. He was killed in battle in 1513.

The first Tudor king, Henry VII, united England under his rule. James IV built a fine fleet of ships.

Henry VIII became king of England in 1509. He married six times. Two of his wives were beheaded.

During the 1500s people argued about religion. Mary I ordered people to be burned at the stake.

# Good Queen Bess!
### last of the Tudors

**Elizabeth I was the daughter of Henry VIII.** She became queen in 1558 and she had her father's temper, as well as his love of music, dancing and fine clothes. Unlike her father, Elizabeth never married. She was also a much wiser ruler than Henry. The last of the Tudors, Elizabeth died in 1603.

BIT TOO MUCH MEAD!

A NICE LAMB KEBAB WITH CHILI SAUCE...

AT YOUR SERVICE, MA'AM.

LAMB? BLEAT!

During Elizabeth's reign, Francis Drake sailed right around the world. Elizabeth made him a knight.

Parts of England grew wealthy as merchants sold cloth across Europe. Mary Queen of Scots was executed.

In the 1590s, theatres grew popular. People crowded into them to see the plays of William Shakespeare.

# Plots and plans

## fireworks!

After Elizabeth I died, the throne passed to James VI of Scotland. James was the son of Mary Queen of Scots. He now also became James I of England. James proved to be an intelligent king who wrote about the dangers of tobacco and introduced a new English translation of the Bible. He was succeeded by his son, Charles I.

In 1605, Guy Fawkes was accused of plotting to blow up the Houses of Parliament. Charles I started a civil w

oliver cromwell was more famous as a football player than as a politician. football didn't have many rules in those days!

Charles I started the Civil War in 1642. He quarrelled with Parliament about religion and taxes. This lead to six years of fighting. Eventually, Charles was put on trial and beheaded. For 11 years, England had no king. At first a Council of State ran the country. Then in 1653 Parliament chose the commander of the Roundheads, Oliver Cromwell, to rule as Lord Protector.

The king's soldiers were Cavaliers and the soldiers of Parliament were Roundheads. The Roundheads won.

# Plague and fire

## dangerous times

KNIT ONE, PURL ONE...

In 1665 the plague, or Black Death, returned to London.

Thousands of people died. The disease was spread by rat fleas, but people didn't know this. City folk fled to the countryside, taking their deadly germs with them. Then in 1666, a spark from a fire set a bakery alight. The Great Fire of London had started.

The Great Fire raged throughout London for five days. Much of the city had to be rebuilt in stone.

When Charles II died in 1665, his brother became James II of England. However James was a Catholic, and the Protestant supporters threw him off the throne. James' daughter became Queen Mary II, ruling jointly with her Protestant husband, William III.

The first cannons did more harm to the soldiers firing them than to the enemy! In 1460, an exploding cannon killed James II of Scotland.

OUT WITH THE OLD!

BUT I'M THE KING!

STAND AND DELIVER!

WHAT? PAPERS? SPEECHES?

James II was thrown off the throne in 1688. During the 1600s and 1700s, highwaymen held up coaches.

# Wealthy and powerful
## Industrial Age

Queen Victoria ruled from 1837 to 1901. During this time, Britain became wealthy and powerful. It was the Industrial Age, and Britain's empire also expanded. However, many people were still desperately poor. They worked in factories, mills and coal mines. Pay was low and work was dangerous.

Queen Victoria also became Empress of India. Many people were so poor they had little or no money.

## can you believe it?

Bathing in the sea became popular in Victorian times. People changed in bathing machines, which were then hauled into the sea!

Cities and factories spread across the Scottish Lowlands, the north of England, the Midlands, South Wales and Northern Ireland. Factories used cotton, rubber and timber from other areas of the empire and produced goods that were shipped around the world.

me people moved to different areas of the empire, which included parts of Africa, Asia and the Americas.

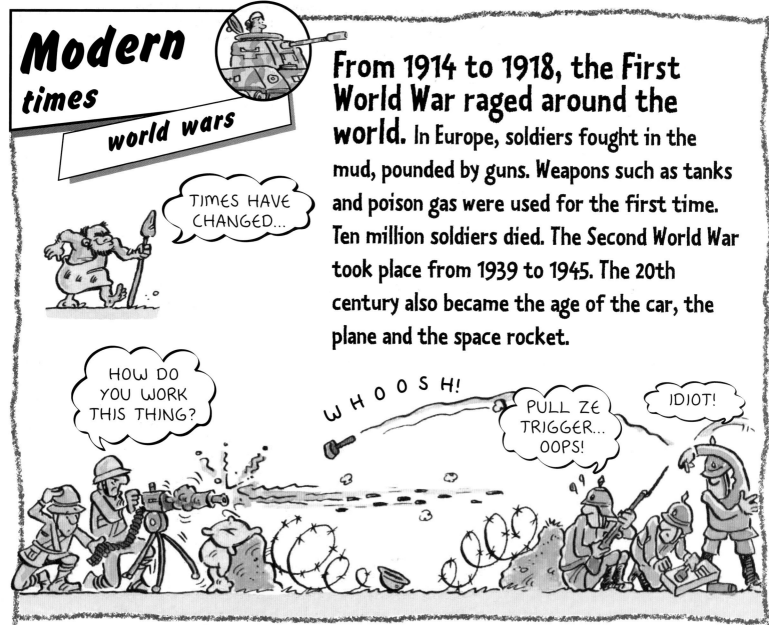

# Modern times

## world wars

**From 1914 to 1918, the First World War raged around the world.** In Europe, soldiers fought in the mud, pounded by guns. Weapons such as tanks and poison gas were used for the first time. Ten million soldiers died. The Second World War took place from 1939 to 1945. The 20th century also became the age of the car, the plane and the space rocket.

During the First World War, the French and English battled against the Germans. Fighting was fierce.

In 1918, women over 30 were given the right to vote. The Second World War was the worst war in history.

Millions of people died during both World Wars. Inventions changed everyone's lives in the 20th century.

# VICTORIAN TIMES

# Queen of an empire
## a new era

Queen Victoria came to the throne in 1837. During her 54-year reign, Britain was transformed by the Industrial Revolution. It became the most powerful nation in the world. The rich became richer than they could ever have dreamed of, but the poor faced terrible poverty.

Victoria's father died when she was a baby. She became queen at 18 and married Prince Albert in 1840.

Victoria and Albert had a happy marriage, and they had nine children. Their names were Vicky, Edward, Alice, Alfred, Helena, Louise, Arthur, Leopold and Beatrice.

British law stated that no man was allowed to propose to the queen, so Victoria had to ask for Albert's hand in marriage!

GOTCHA.

GEEK!

DARNED KIDS ARE A NIGHTMARE...

THAT'S DISGUSTING!

DON'T BE RUDE, ARTHUR!

Victoria and Albert valued family life. Unfortunately, three of their children died before Victoria did.

**The poor lived in tiny, dirty terraced houses.** They rarely had running water and one house was often home to a family of ten. For the rich, Victorian Britain was a wonderful place to live. They wore expensive clothes and went to the theatre.

Poor families had to live in cramped, dirty conditions. Brothers and sisters had to share a bed.

People began to demand the right to vote. In the 1840s in Ireland, thousands died from starvation.

The rich wore fabulous clothes and expensive jewellery. They flocked to musicals and lavish events.

# Work and no play

## job search

Factories and mills provided employment for the Victorian poor. People worked all day with dangerous machinery, making goods to sell around the world. In small clothing factories called sweatshops, workers were hustled into cramped, dingy rooms to work from dawn to dusk – earning barely enough money to survive.

By the 1850s printing had been mechanized. Mining was one of the deadliest jobs in Victorian Britain.

Florence Nightingale was a nurse who cared for soldiers during Crimean War. She became known as the 'lady with the lamp'.

Miners faced the constant threat of unstable shafts and explosive gases. To check for gas, miners often took canaries to work with them. If the birds stopped singing, it was seen as a sign that gas was present. In 1842 the Mines Act was passed, banning children from working in mines.

SWEEP THAT CHIMNEY SHARPISH!

SWEAT!!

RING!

APPLES AND PEARS...

DING!

WHAT'RE YOU SELLING? STAIRS?

ys were sent up chimneys to sweep them clean. Pedlars tried to sell their wares, such as rags, on the street.

# Wicked workhouses

## a miserable life

**Workhouses were supposed to encourage the poor to be less reliant on hand-outs.** So in order to receive poor relief, such as food or clothes, people had to live in workhouses. The conditions in these places were terrible. People were starving and cold, and children were often beaten.

Food in the workhouse consisted of watery soup called gruel, and a little bread and cheese.

The writer Charles Dickens was so shocked by the conditions of workhouses that he wrote *Oliver Twist* to highlight the problem. Dickens campaigned throughout his lifetime to turn public opinion against these terrible places.

Rich ladies wore corsets made of whalebone, strengthened with steel! These gave them a tiny waist but must have been agony to wear.

WHEN I GET OUT OF HERE...

I'LL KNOCK HIS BLOCK OFF!

YIKES!!

CHILDREN SHOULD BE SEEN AND NOT HEARD.

SO SHOULD SOME ADULTS!

Children were beaten for misbehaving and many ended up in hospital as a result of their punishment.

# Bright ideas

## clever clogs!

CAN'T YOU KNOCK FIRST?

**The Victorians were full of clever ideas.** Prince Albert was so impressed with these ideas and inventions that he decided to hold the Great Exhibition to show them off. In 1851 thousands of people gathered in the newly built Crystal Palace to show off their gadgets to the dazzled public.

I MADE IT ALL BY MYSELF.

CLEVER BOY!

CREEP!

Crystal Palace was three times the length of St Paul's cathedral and covered 26 acres.

William Cook and Charles Wheatstone invented the Victorian internet – the electric telegraph. In 1837 they started to send messages down metal lines using electricity. In 1866 telegraph lines were laid under the Atlantic Ocean all the way to Canada.

The Victorian Age also saw the first dentist's drill and the first porcelain false teeth!

OOCH! OUCH!

ZZ ZZ!!

BLING!

EUREKA!

YOU SOUND LIKE A BABE!

YOU CHARMER! BET YOU'RE GORGEOUS TOO!

Swan invented the lightbulb in 1860, and the telephone arrived in 1876. Photography also became popular.

**Victorian steam trains hurtled along tracks.** By 1900, 35,000 kilometres of track had been laid in Britain. One of the most famous routes ran from the West Country to London and was designed by Isambard Kingdom Brunel (1806–1859). Passengers were so impressed that the railway was nicknamed 'God's Wonderful Railway'.

HORSE PLAY!

WHEN I SAID LUXURY TRAIN I MEANT ORIENT EXPRESS!

WISH I'D BROUGHT MY SAILOR'S OUTFIT!

PUFF! PUFF! PUFF!

Brunel also designed *The Great Western*, the biggest ship in the world of its time. It reached the USA in 183

## can you believe it?

Some people thought that travelling on the fastest Victorian trains would lead to death by suffocation!

Isambard Kingdom Brunel was a brilliant engineer. He is famous for his designs of railways, bridges, tunnels and great ocean liners. *The Great Western* was the first steamship to take part in transatlantic service. Brunel went on to design two more great steamships – *The Great Britain* and *The Great Eastern*.

In 1853, George Cayley flew a glider 200 metres. The first practical cars appeared in 1895.

# And... relax

## winding down

**Thanks to the arrival of railways, holidays became available to the Victorian public.** People loved trips to the seaside, and resorts such as Blackpool and Brighton became popular holiday spots. Educated young men and women travelled abroad to places such as Switzerland and Italy, visiting sights such as Mount Vesuvius.

Wealthy people used bathing machines. These were horse-drawn huts that were wheeled into the sea.

Funfairs first became popular in Victorian times, with a variety of steam-powered rides.

People in towns and cities loved going to music halls. These were large rooms built at the side of pubs. Here, people could watch simple plays, or entertainers such as singers and dancers. Marie Lloyd was one of the most famous entertainers and was given the nickname Queen of the Music Hall.

WHOOSSHHHHH!

HE'S A BUNDLE OF LAUGHS!

HANDBALL! REF!

FLYING TRUNK! LOOK OUT!

e professional football league was formed. Tossing the caber (tree trunk) was part of the Highland Games.

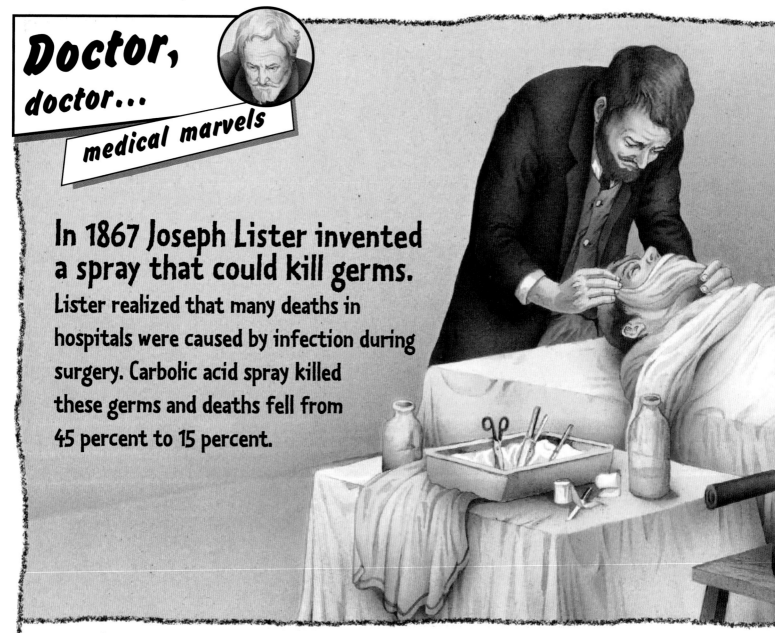

In 1867 Joseph Lister invented a spray that could kill germs.
Lister realized that many deaths in hospitals were caused by infection during surgery. Carbolic acid spray killed these germs and deaths fell from 45 percent to 15 percent.

Operating theatres became much cleaner and safer with the use of carbolic acid spray.

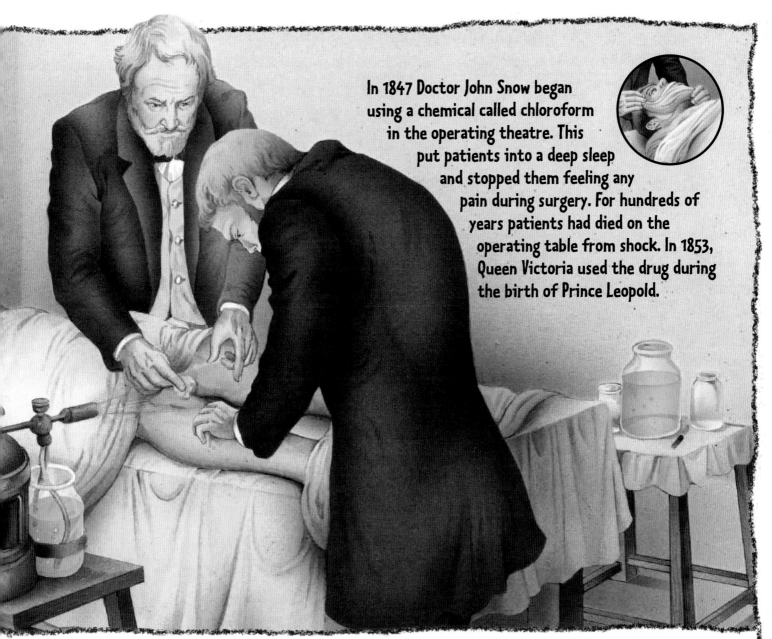

In 1847 Doctor John Snow began using a chemical called chloroform in the operating theatre. This put patients into a deep sleep and stopped them feeling any pain during surgery. For hundreds of years patients had died on the operating table from shock. In 1853, Queen Victoria used the drug during the birth of Prince Leopold.

Chloroform put patients into a deep sleep. This meant people didn't experience pain during surgery.

# Building blocks

## great architects

'Gothic' was a style of architecture very popular in Victorian times. Buildings with pointed arches and high spires sprung up all over the land. The most famous examples of Gothic architecture are the new Houses of Parliament, the University of Glasgow and St Pancras station in London.

The new Houses of Parliament replaced the Palace of Westminster when it burned down in 1834.

The Victorians loved to build with iron and glass. Iron bridges spanned rivers, such as the Forth Rail Bridge in Scotland. Probably the most famous iron and glass building was the Crystal Palace, which housed the Great Exhibition in 1851.

Greek-style architecture became popular in Scotland. Four churches were built in this style by Alexander 'Greek' Thomson.

In 1897, work began on the Glasgow School of Art building. The architect was Charles Rennie Mackintosh.

# Glorious food

## dinner time!

**Victorian cooks had a problem keeping food fresh.** Meat or fish would go off quickly unless it was kept cool. Then in 1900 the first refrigerator was invented. Scientists also found a way to put food in to tins, meaning that groceries such as fruit and vegetables could be kept fresh for months.

Cooks worked very hard. All food was prepared by hand. The arrival of ice cream delighted children!

Exotic fruits such as pineapple and kiwi were enjoyed by the wealthy. Spices from India became popular.

Milkmen carried large pails of milk, which was delivered straight from the farm to people's doors.

FINDERS KEEPERS!

By 1856, most towns and cities had their own police force. The first policemen were known as 'peelers' or 'bobbies'. This was after Sir Robert Peel, who set up London's Metropolitan police force in 1829. Policemen had wooden truncheons to help defend themselves against criminals.

OI! GET BACK HERE, YOU TEA LEAF!

FINE MESS THIS IS!

GULP!

Policemen wore blue tailcoats and reinforced top hats. This helped people to recognize them.

In 1884 fingerprints were first used to identify criminals. Soon after, detectives learned how to spot tiny specks of blood. There were also new methods for detecting the use of poison, one of the most common forms of murder.

People were so gripped by Sir Arthur Conan Doyle's stories about the detective Sherlock Holmes, they thought he was real!

ONE FOR THE ALBUM?

HIC! WASH THAT?

GOTCHA!

LOSER!

HA! HA! WHEN I SAID LET'S PLAY HANGMAN...

GULP!

BLING!

Science helped to solve crimes – but pickpockets were still rife. Fewer people were sentenced to death.

# School rules

*teacher's pet!*

In 1880 a new law meant that all children between the ages of five and ten had to go to school. However, education wasn't free, so few children could afford to attend. Then in 1891 the law was changed, and school became free for all children up to the age of 11.

Lessons focused on the 'three Rs' – Reading, wRiting and aRithmetic. Children learned by repeating lines.

Many working-class children had to work all week, and had little chance to learn. Sunday or Charity Schools were set up to try to give these children a basic education. They were taught how to read and write and they also attended Bible study classes.

The most famous pickpocket is the Artful Dodger, a character in Dickens' novel *Oliver Twist*.

OOPS! NO SHOES!

SORRY WE'RE LATE!

DING! DING!

DETENTION FOR YOU TWO!

THE SHAME OF IT!

If a pupil was poor at a lesson, they would have to stand in a corner and wear the dunce's cap.

# Family life

## home sweet home

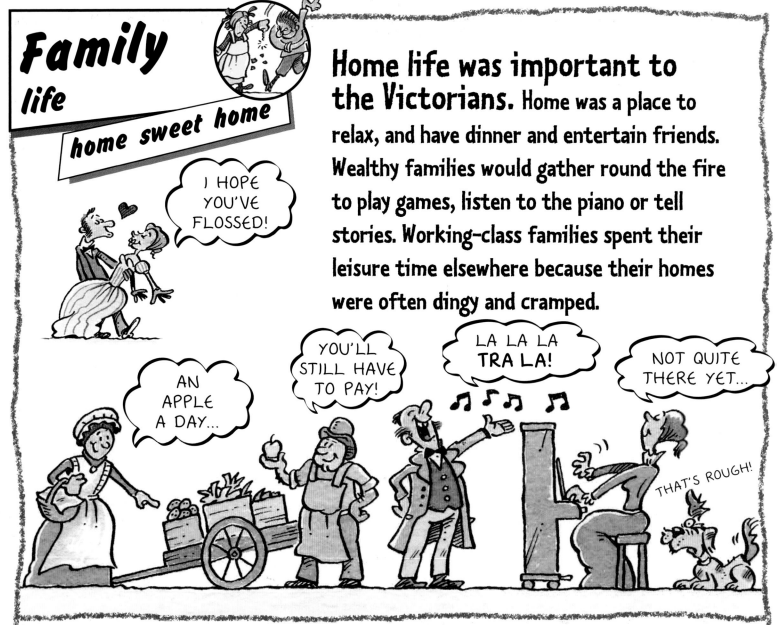

**Home life was important to the Victorians.** Home was a place to relax, and have dinner and entertain friends. Wealthy families would gather round the fire to play games, listen to the piano or tell stories. Working-class families spent their leisure time elsewhere because their homes were often dingy and cramped.

Poor families would eat from cheap food stalls. Everyone loved crowding round the piano for a sing-song.

Naughty children were not tolerated. Rich parents employed nannies to care for their children.

Children had toys such as hobby horses and yo-yos. They also played games such as snakes and ladders.

# Telling tales

## great authors

The most famous storyteller in Victorian Britain was Charles Dickens. He was fascinated by the poor areas of London and would pound the streets at night, making notes of what he saw. The Brontë sisters went on to become some of the greatest writers of the Victorian age.

Perhaps Dickens, most famous novel is *Oliver Twist*. The Brontës were raised on the bleak Yorkshire Moors.

When Queen Victoria died, people wore black. Iron fences were given a fresh coat of black paint, too.

Robert Louis Stevenson could write with astonishing speed. The scottish novelist wrote *The Strange Case of Doctor Jekyll and Mr Hyde* – a story of a troubled doctor who turns into Mr Hyde, a nasty character, after drinking a potion. Stevenson also wrote *Treasure Island* and *Kidnapped*, all about pirate adventures.

Robert Louis Stevenson wrote several famous novels. *Alice in Wonderland* was written by Lewis Carroll.

# QUIZ TIME!

Think you know everything there is to know about British history? Try these quiz questions to test your knowledge. Use the picture clues to help you, or look back in the book.

# Roman Invaders

1. What did Celtic warriors use for speedy attacks?

2. In what year did Julius Caesar first land in Britain?

Question 1

3. In AD60, who did the Romans attack?

Question 3

4. Which queen attacked Colchester, London and St Albans?

5. What was the capital city of Britannia?

Question 4

6. What system did the Romans introduce that wasn't improved until the 1800s?

Question 6

7. What were aqueducts?

8. Who was the Roman goddess of love?

9. How long was Hadrian's Wall?

Question 8

10. What were villa floors decorated with?

11. What did children learn at school?

Question 11

12. What modern board game is similar to 'Three Stones'?

13. Which trades were a speciality of the Celts?

14. What was the name of the robe worn by important men?

Question 14

15. How many courses would there be at a banquet?

Question 15

# Kings and Queens

1. Which queen rebelled against the Romans?

2. What did King Cnut try to command?

3. Which king argued with Thomas Becket?

4. Who owned Britain's first zoo?

5. In 1348, which terrible disease reached England?

Question 2

Question 4

6. In what year did Richard III die?

7. Was Henry VIII a Tudor or a Stewart?

8. How many wives did Henry VIII have?

Question 8

9. Who was the daughter of Anne Boleyn?

10. Elizabeth I ordered which queen to be executed?

11. When was the Battle of Hastings?

12. Who was known as the 'Young Pretender'?

Question 9

Question 12

13. Which king wanted to be a farmer?

14. How many children did Queen Victoria have?

15. When Prince Philip married, what new title was he given?

Question 13

Question 14

# British History

1. What kind of stone did early Britons use to make tools?

2. When was Stonehenge built?

3. Who started to settle in the British Isles around 600BC?

4. Did the Romans conquer all of Scotland?

5. What name did the Romans give to their luxurious country homes?

Question 1

Question 5

Question 3

Question 6

6. Angles, Saxons, Jutes and Frisians became know as who?

7. Which king ruled the kingdom of Wessex from 871 to 899?

Question 9

8. Where did the Vikings come from?

9. What was a berserkir?

10. In 1066, who defeated King Harold at the Battle of Hastings?

11. What is the name for the water-filled ditch around a castle?

Question 12

12. In the Middle Ages, what protected many small towns?

13. Who was the first Tudor king?

14. Which king had six wives?

15. During the reign of Elizabeth I, who sailed right around the world?

16. Which playwright became famous in the 1590s?

Question 13

Question 15

17. In 1605, who was accused of plotting to blow up the Houses of Parliament?

18. Who were the Roundheads and Cavaliers?

19. Where did the Great Fire of London begin?

Question 17

Question 19

Question 20

20. Where did poor Victorian people work?

21. What was Queen Victoria's title in India?

22. During the First World War, who did the French and English battle against?

23. In 1918, what were women over 30 given the right to do?

Question 22

## Answers

1. Flint   2. Between 3000 and 1500BC   3. The Celts   4. North Scotland wasn't conquered   5. Villa   6. Anglo-Saxons   7. King Alfred   8. Norway, Sweden and Denmark   9. Viking warrior   10. William Duke of Normandy   11. Moat   12. Castle   13. Henry VII   14. Henry VIII   15. Francis Drake   16. William Shakespeare   17. Guy Fawkes   18. Soldiers in the Civil War   19. In a bakery   20. Factories, mills and coalmines   21. Empress   22. The Germans   23. Vote

# Victorian Times

**1. When did Queen Victoria come to the throne?**

Question 2

**2. Florence Nightingale became known as who?**

**3. Which book, written by Charles Dickens, highlighted the conditions of workhouses?**

Question 3

**4. When was the Great Exhibition held?**

**5. Who designed the *Great Western* ship?**

Question 5

Question 6

6. Which seaside towns became popular holiday resorts?

7. Who was 'Queen of the Music Hall'?

8. What was invented by Joseph Lister?

9. In what year did the Palace of Westminster burn down?

Question 9

10. Who was Charles Rennie Mackintosh?

11. The arrival of which food delighted Victorian children?

Question 11

12. What was a 'peeler'?

13. What did children study at school?

14. In the novel *Oliver Twist*, what kind of person was the Artful Dodger?

15. What was a hobby horse?

Question 12

Question 13

Question 15

# Index

# Index

# Index

# Index